Amazing
Animal Defenses

Animals with
Awesome Armor
Shells, Scales, and Exoskeletons

Susan K. Mitchell

Enslow Publishers, Inc.
40 Industrial Road
Box 398
Berkeley Heights, NJ 07922
USA
    http://www.enslow.com

These books are dedicated to Emily, who inspired the author.

Library of Congress Cataloging-in-Publication Data
Mitchell, Susan K.
  Animals with awesome armor : shells, scales, and exoskeletons / Susan K. Mitchell.
      p. cm. — (Amazing animal defenses)
  Includes bibliographical references and index.
  Summary: "Readers will learn how animals such as armadillos and crabs protect themselves from predators"—Provided by publisher.
  ISBN 978-0-7660-3296-5
  1. Armored animals—Juvenile literature. I. Title.
  QL940.M58 2009
  591.47'7—dc22

                                        2008011456

ISBN-10: 0-7660-3296-5

Printed in the United States of America

10 9 8 7 6 5 4 3 2 1

To Our Readers:
We have done our best to make sure all Internet Addresses in this book were active and appropriate when we went to press. However, the author and the publisher have no control over and assume no liability for the material available on those Internet sites or on other Web sites they may link to. Any comments or suggestions can be sent by e-mail to comments@enslow.com or to the address on the back cover.

♻ Enslow Publishers, Inc., is committed to printing our books on recycled paper. The paper in every book contains 10% to 30% post-consumer waste (PCW). The cover board on the outside of each book contains 100% PCW. Our goal is to do our part to help young people and the environment too!

Cover photo: JJMaree/iStockphoto
Interior photos: Alamy/blickwinkel, pp. 7, 13, 34, 36, 38; Alamy/Peter Titmuss, p. 14; Alamy/Terry Whittaker, p. 17; Alamy/Nick Greaves, p. 26; Alamy/Jeff Rotman, p. 32; Alamy/Paul David Drabble, p. 44; Animals Animals–Earth Scenes/Mark Jones, p. 10; Animals Animals–Earth Scenes/Fabio Colombini Medeiros, p. 16; Animals Animals–Earth Scenes/Doug Wechsler, p. 29; Animals Animals–Earth Scenes/Franklin Viola, p. 30; Animals Animals–Earth Scenes/David M. Dennis, p. 37; Courtesy of Jerry F. Butler and Donald W. Hall, University of Florida, p. 40 (top and bottom); iStockphoto/JJMaree, p. 1; iStockphoto/winhorse, p. 4; iStockphoto/Robert Frith, p. 9; iStockphoto/Jody Dingle, p. 18; iStockphoto/Liz Leyden, p. 19; iStockphoto/Laure Neish, p. 21; iStockphoto/Alan Tobey, p. 22; iStockphoto/Matt Abbe, p. 24; iStockphoto/Andrea Gingerich, p. 25; iStockphoto/lisinski, p. 28; iStockphoto/Geoff Hardy, p. 33; iStockphoto/Alena Yakusheva, p. 42; iStockphoto/Craig DeBourbon, p. 43.

Contents

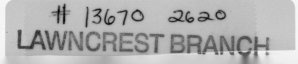

Chapter 1 No Ordinary Knights

In the middle ages, knights wore heavy, metal armor. It protected them in battle. But even then, wearing armor was not a new idea. Animals had been using armor to protect themselves for millions of years. Animal armor comes in many forms. Some animals have thick shells. Others have tough skin. Still other animals have bony armor.

◀ **Turtles have some of the best armor in the animal world. It is made of bone.**

Armor can be made of many things, but bone is one of the toughest types of armor. Bones are strong enough to make up the skeleton inside humans and many animals. They can also be a tough covering on the outside. Bony armor is not part of the skeleton. Instead, it is usually connected to the outside of an animal's skin. That means that the animal cannot crawl out of its armor. Turtles are one type of animal with this kind of armor.

The great thing about bony armor is that it lasts forever. It is the only suit of armor the animal will ever need. An animal with armor made of bone never has to grow new armor. Bone armor grows with the animal. But even tough bony armor has weaknesses. For example, bone has nerve endings. This means that an animal with bony armor can feel pressure and pain if the armor is damaged.

The Science of Armor

Bony armor is often covered in keratin. That is the same type of material that makes up human fingernails. Keratin by itself is also a kind of armor. It grows like bony armor, but is much softer than bone. It bends easily. Many reptiles have scales made of keratin. Snake scales might not seem like armor, but they can be very tough.

Many insects and crabs have armor made of chitin. This type of armor is often called an exoskeleton. It is very strong, but unlike bone, it does not grow. Animals with chitin armor have to keep growing new armor. As the animal grows, their old armor splits and the animal sheds it. This is called molting. Underneath is a new suit of chitin armor ready to protect the animal. Some animals may molt many times during their life.

Some animal armor also contains calcium carbonate. This is a mineral found in shelled sea

Wild FACT A few armored animals have sharp, thorny growths on their armor. They can use these as weapons against predators.

A snake's scales are made of keratin. It is the same material that human fingernails are made of.

animals and snails. An animal with this type of armor grows its own shell. Its body makes the calcium carbonate, which forms a shell around the animal. This makes the armor harder, stiffer, and stronger than armor made only from chitin. Animals with this type of armor do not have to molt. They just keep adding calcium to their shell. This way, the shell grows with the animal.

Back to the Stone Age

Animal armor has been around for millions of years. Some of the most well-known rough and tough armored animals were the dinosaurs. But just because they were big did not mean they were always safe. Many dinosaurs were in danger of being eaten by even bigger ones. Plant-eating dinosaurs were especially at risk.

Getting Medieval

There are many animals with armor. It may be special skin, scales, or bone. But none of them have metal-plated armor like medieval knights. That is, until now. Scientists found an ocean snail that actually has armor made of metal! The discovery of this snail is so new that scientists have not even given the snail a name yet.

The snail lives deep in the Indian Ocean. It lives near hydrothermal vents. These are cracks in the ocean floor where super-heated water bursts through. It is usually heated by the red-hot magma flowing just beneath the surface of the ocean floor.

The snail's special armor is made up of two types of iron metal. Iron is found in the waters near hydrothermal vents. Scientists believe the snail absorbs the iron from the water. The snail's metal scales also make it magnetic. When scientists studied the snail, it kept sticking to their metal tools!

They could be huge but usually did not have sharp claws or teeth for defense. Instead, they had hard, bony plates or super-thick skin for protection.

Many of today's armored animals can trace their history back even before the age of the dinosaurs.

When insects such as the dragonfly outgrow their armor, they climb out and leave it behind (right).

Over millions of years, their armor has not changed much. That is because the same kind of armor that protected them millions of years ago still works well today.

Armor is a good defense, but it is not perfect. Many predators have figured out how to get past their prey's armor. Sometimes armor is no match for sharp teeth. Animal armor can also be broken. However, it is still a great defense to have in an animal-eat-animal world!

Chapter 2

Strike Up the Bands

There are many armored animals in the world. Most of them are insects, reptiles, or sea animals. The armadillo is an unusual armored animal, however, because it is a mammal. Most mammals have furry bodies. The armadillo does have a little bit of fur. Yet, in addition to the skin and fur it is covered in armor.

The armadillo's armor is called a carapace. It is not a solid shell like a turtle's.

Armadillos usually have three, six, or nine bands of armor. This is a six-banded armadillo.

An armadillo's armor is made up of sections called bands. Armadillos are grouped by how many bands of armor they have—usually three, six, or nine. The bands are made up of bone. The bony bands overlap each other. They are covered with hard scales made of keratin.

The word armadillo means "little armored one" in Spanish. There are more than twenty types of armadillos. Some, such as the giant armadillo, are the size of a large dog. Others, such as the pink fairy armadillo, are tiny— only about six inches long.

The most common one is the nine-banded armadillo. It can be found all over South America. It is also very easy to find in the southeastern United States, especially in Texas and Florida. Since armor does not help keep an armadillo's body very warm, they live in warm areas.

WILD FACT

Armadillos are most closely related to sloths and anteaters.

Dig It!

Armadillos are born diggers. From the moment they are born, they have the need to dig. An armadillo's body is perfect for digging. It is low to the ground. Its legs are very short. On the end of an armadillo's front legs are huge, strong claws.

These claws are good for digging for food. Armadillos eat mostly insects. They also sometimes eat roots or bird eggs. Armadillos have even been known to nibble on dead animals. They have very small eyes and do not see well. They use their flat snout and claws to push along the ground looking for a bite to eat.

While an armadillo's sight and hearing may be bad, its sense of smell is super. An armadillo can smell a tasty treat that is several inches under the ground. When an armadillo finds food, it starts digging. It uses a long, sticky tongue to grab the food. The armadillo's tongue does most of the work

▼ **An armadillo's claws are designed for digging. It spends most of its time burrowing and digging for food.**

when eating. It grabs insects or bites of other food. It also mashes up the food before the armadillo swallows. Anything that cannot be mashed by the tongue gets ground up by the armadillo's teeth.

Armadillos also dig to make burrows. Unlike some burrowing animals that may only have one or two burrows, an armadillo might have many. Some burrows are used as a living area. Others are used to escape danger. Armadillos also dig burrows to keep warm during cooler weather. They may even

13

Tipping the Scales

Armadillos are not the only mammal with armor. **The pangolin (PANG-ga-lin) of Africa has even tougher scaly armor. This animal is also called a scaly anteater. These strange creatures live very much like armadillos. Pangolins dig to find food. They also live in burrows.**

The armor of the pangolin is also a lot like an armadillo's. It is made of many hard overlapping scales. The scales are made of keratin just like an armadillo's.

There is one huge difference between the scales of a pangolin and an armadillo, however. The pangolin's scales are razor sharp! When frightened, it rolls itself into a tight ball. The armor not only protects the pangolin's body, but is a weapon also.

The super-sharp edges of these scales would cut any predator that tried to pry open the pangolin.

share burrows with other animals such as rabbits or skunks.

Having a Ball

Most of the time, the armadillo's armor keeps it safe. Unfortunately, it is not a perfect defense. The armor covers only the armadillo's head, shoulders, and back. Sometimes it also covers the tail. The armadillo's belly, however, is not protected at all.

WILDFACT **The female nine-banded armadillo usually gives birth to four identical babies at once (also known as quadruplets).**

The first thing an armadillo does when it feels threatened is hide or run away. It may try to dig into the ground very quickly. If there is no time to dig, it will lie close to the ground instead. This is a way to try to protect its soft belly and legs.

The three-banded armadillo can protect its belly in a very interesting way. Its bands of armor are very flexible. They allow the armadillo to curl up into a tight ball. It pulls its legs close to its body. It tucks its head and tail inside also.

The pink fairy armadillo has another strange way of protecting itself. This tiny armadillo has a hard plate covering its rear-end. When in danger, the pink fairy armadillo dives headfirst into a burrow. Its rear plate acts like a shield.

The nine-banded armadillo is one of the few armadillos that can swim away from danger.

▼ Some types of armadillos protect their unarmored bellies by rolling themselves up into a little ball.

Hey Honey, What's for Dinner?

Some mammals have super-tough skin that acts like a sort of armor. The honey badger is one of them. This South African animal is a carnivore. That means it eats mostly meat. One if its favorite treats is bee larvae. These baby bees are found inside honey-filled beehives—that is where the honey badger gets its name.

Getting into a beehive is a very risky activity, but the honey badger is protected against bee stings. It has thick, rubbery skin that acts like armor. Honey badgers can put up with hundreds of bee stings while going after the bee larvae in a hive.

It can fill its stomach with air and float away. It can also hold its breath and walk along the bottom of a stream or river. The nine-banded armadillo can hold its breath for a very long time. These tiny armored tanks can be full of tricks.

17

Chapter 3

Mighty and Mobile

Most turtles are neither teenage, mutant, nor
ninjas. Turtles are, however, some of the oldest
armored animals in the world. They have lived
on Earth for millions of years. In all that time,
they have changed very little. That is because
their shelled body protects them so well.

Turtles can be called many things. This
usually depends on where they live. The name
turtle usually refers to the animals that live in

◀ Turtles can live on land or in water. They have changed very little in millions of years.

water. They have flipper-like legs and feet that help them swim. Tortoise (TOR-tus) is the name used for turtles that usually live only on land. Their shell is more dome-shaped than the flatter turtle shell. Tortoises also have rounder, thicker legs and feet than turtles. Somewhere in between are the terrapins. These animals can live equally in water and on land.

No matter what you call theses animals, they are all reptiles. That is the same class of

▲ The tortoise is a type of turtle that spends most of its life on land. Instead of flippers for swimming, it has feet for walking.

animals as snakes and lizards. In fact, turtles are the only reptile with a shell for protection.

Pick Up the Carapace

A turtle's shell is made up of two parts. The top part is the carapace. The bottom part is called the plastron. Unlike an armadillo, a turtle's belly is also protected. The whole shell is attached to the turtle's backbone and ribs.

Wild FACT **Turtles can breathe through their bottoms! The opening at their rear end is called a cloaca (klo-AY-ka). Turtles can suck water into this opening. Then they can absorb oxygen from the water.**

The shell is made of very hard bone and is covered in plates of keratin called scutes. The shell is not one large bone, however. It is actually made up of 50 to 60 bones that are joined together. Just like the bones of any

Most turtles can pull their legs and head into their shell for extra protection.

animal, the shell grows with the turtle. A turtle has its shell for its whole life.

Only the turtle's head, legs, and tail are not covered by its shell. To protect these areas, most types of turtles have retractable body parts. This means that they can pull their legs and head inside their shell. Other turtles can only pull their long necks to the side. Then their head fits neatly under the front of the shell. Box turtles have a special muscle in their plastron. They can use this muscle like a hinge to close the top and bottom shells tightly together. Sea turtles are the only turtles that cannot pull themselves into their shells.

A Weak Spot in Their Armor

While turtle eggs and babies face a lot of danger, **most adult turtles have few predators. The biggest threat to any type of turtle are humans. Many turtles die every year due to human carelessness. Some are hit by cars. Many are killed by fishermen. Others are kept as pets by people who do not know how to care for them properly. In these cases, no amount of armor can protect a turtle.**

A turtle's shell is great protection from predators. It also helps a turtle in other ways. A sea turtle's smooth, flat shell helps it dive and swim. A large, domed shell like that of the Galapagos tortoise helps shade the turtle from the hot sun. Many shells also blend in with the turtle's environment to help it hide.

WILD FACT A leatherback is a type of sea turtle that has leathery skin that covers its shell. It does not have scutes like most sea turtles.

Slow, Steady, and Safe

Since turtles are reptiles, they lay eggs. After female turtles lay their eggs, most of them leave the nest. This means that baby turtles are on their own from the moment they hatch. Hatching is dangerous business for a baby turtle. Even with their small shells, they are almost defenseless. Many baby turtles are eaten by predators before they have a chance to leave the nest.

23

School of Hard Knocks

A few other animals carry around an armored mobile home. Snails, like turtles, have a shell to protect them. Also like turtles, a snail has its shell for its whole life. A snail's shell keeps growing as the snail grows. It is not made of bone like a turtle's shell, however. It is made of calcium carbonate. That is the same mineral used to make chalk.

Snails have a very soft body. When frightened, they pull their body inside their shell. This makes it harder for predators to eat them. Unfortunately, a snail's shell is not as tough as a turtle's. Most predators have learned that a snail's shell is easy to break. They simply smash the shell to get to the snail inside.

Baby leatherbacks and other baby turtles have shells, but face a lot of danger. They are small and usually have no adult turtle around to protect them.

For the lucky babies who survive, growing up to adulthood can take a very long time. Some turtles live to be more than 100 years old. As they grow, the turtles' armor keeps growing and protecting them.

But wherever they go, they go slowly. It is a good thing that their suit of armor is always there to keep them safe.

Chapter 4

Feeling Crabby

One of the coolest armored "crabs" is not a crab at all! It is the horseshoe crab. More closely related to ticks, spiders, or scorpions, the horseshoe crab looks like a walking helmet. It is called a horseshoe crab because people once believed it was a crab. Also, it is shaped like a horse's hoof.

Horseshoe crabs are not crabs at all. They are a well-armored relative of spiders!

These animals have changed very little over millions of years. Whatever they are doing, they are doing it right. There has been no need for them to change.

The tough shell of a horseshoe crab is made of chitin. This is the same type of material that also makes up the hard outer covering of many insects. Unlike keratin or bone, chitin does not grow. That means that animals with shells of chitin must molt. The horseshoe crab molts several times during its first years of life.

When a horseshoe crab molts, the old shell splits open and the horseshoe crab crawls out of it. Until the new shell underneath hardens, the horseshoe crab is very soft. It has no armor and is in danger. During this time, horseshoe crabs hide in the mud. Each time a

WILD FACT Female horseshoe crabs are bigger than the males. An average female is about 12 inches wide, while an average male is about 8 inches wide.

A horseshoe crab's abandoned suit of chitin armor is a common sight on the beach.

horseshoe crab grows a new set of armor, it is bigger than the last. It takes from seven to ten years for a horseshoe crab to reach its full size. Then it stops molting.

Bending Over Backward

There are four types of horseshoe crabs. Three of them are found off the coast of Asia. The other type lives along the east coast of North

28

America. Horseshoe crabs spend most of their time waddling along the ocean floor.

A horseshoe crab's body has three parts. The large part in the front that includes the head is called the cephalothorax. Behind that is the abdomen. The last part is a very long, sharp tail called a telson. A horseshoe crab's armor has two different parts—one that covers the front area, and another that covers the back area.

▼ **Horseshoe crabs come ashore to spawn, or lay their eggs. A female might lay thousands of tiny eggs at once.**

Clam Up!

Mollusks are sea animals with armor. They have thick shells covering their soft bodies. One type of mollusk has two shells. These are called bivalves. Clams, oysters, and scallops are all bivalves. Their shells are held together by one or two very strong muscles.

One of the biggest armored bivalves is the giant clam. These huge animals can weigh more than 500 pounds. Even with its enormous size, the soft body of a giant clam would be in danger without its armor.

The two pieces of armor are hooked together by a hinge. This lets the horseshoe crab bend in the middle. Being able to bend helps it dig. It also helps the horseshoe crab do a flip. That is handy if it gets washed onto its back by a wave. The horseshoe crab bends in the middle and uses its tail to flip itself armor-side up.

30

The Original Blue-bloods

One of the most unique things about horseshoe crabs is their blood—it can turn blue! Unlike human blood, a horseshoe crab's blood has copper in it. The copper causes the blood to turn blue if it is exposed to air.

The blood of a horseshoe crab can also protect it against germs. If the horseshoe crab gets wounded, the blood forms a hard plug called a clot. The clot keeps the horseshoe crab from getting a serious infection.

Scientists use horseshoe crab blood to test for dangerous germs in many places. They use the blood to test some medicines and medical equipment for safety. If the blue horseshoe crab blood forms a clot on the material being tested, scientists know that the material is not safe for humans. Horseshoe crabs are not hurt or killed for their blood. Only a small amount of their blood is taken by scientists. Then the horseshoe crabs are released back into the ocean.

Scientists collect blood from horseshoe crabs and use it to test for possible germs in medicines and other places. The crabs are not harmed at all.

Even a horseshoe crab's armor is important to humans. The chitin that forms the armor is also used by scientists. They use chitin to make special threads called sutures. These threads are used by doctors to sew up cuts and wounds. Cuts sewn up by the special chitin thread heal much faster than normal. Horseshoe crab chitin is also used to make bandages for burn victims. That is truly amazing armor!

Try This on for Size

Some armored animals are not born with super-tough armor. Instead, they find ways to improve what they have. Hermit crabs, for example, use the armor of other shelled animals for extra protection.

Hermit crabs have an exoskeleton, but it is not quite tough enough to really protect the hermit crab. To stay safe, they use abandoned snail shells as armor. When a snail dies or is eaten by a predator, the empty shell is left behind. It makes the perfect home for a growing hermit crab. It holds the shell in place with its back legs. When the hermit crab grows too big for the shell it is using, it simply crawls out and finds a new one.

Chapter 5

On a Roll

What has a lot of legs, tough armor, and can roll? That is not some silly joke. The answer is a millipede! This animal is covered in a hard outer skin for protection. This hard skin is called an exoskeleton. Many insects have exoskeletons. The millipede is not an insect, however. It belongs to a group of animals called diplopods. That word means "double legged."

    Millipedes have many body parts. These parts are called segments. Each segment has two pairs of legs attached to it—that is where

A millipede's body is made of many segments. The segments are covered with tough armor.

the name diplopod comes in. The number of segments depends on the size of the millipede. The smallest millipede is only about an inch long. These small millipedes usually have around six or seven body segments. The largest millipede in the world is the giant African millipede. It can grow to be more than a foot long! This huge millipede can have several hundred legs. That means a lot of segments!

The name millipede means "thousand foot." The millipede has many legs, but nowhere near a thousand. Most millipedes have only several hundred. The centipede ("hundred foot") is a close cousin of the millipede.

Wild FACT Gross but true: Some millipedes eat their food twice. After they eat once, they turn around and eat their own droppings! Some will even lay their eggs in a nest made of their own droppings.

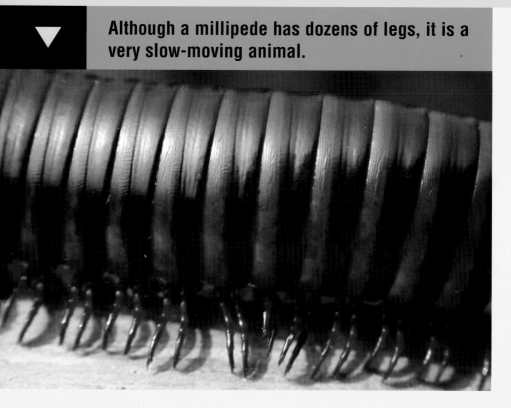

Although a millipede has dozens of legs, it is a very slow-moving animal.

Having so many legs means a millipede can move fast, right? Wrong! The millipede is actually a slow-moving animal. Because of this, it needs its tough armor to protect itself from predators. Many animals love to eat a millipede for a meal.

Beyond Being Tough

Baby millipedes hatch after several weeks inside an egg. Then they go through a second life stage called a nymph. They will keep growing during this stage. The millipede's armor does not grow with its body. As a millipede grows, it molts. Each time it molts, the millipede grows more segments and legs. Most millipedes will molt many times before they become adults.

Many predators search for millipedes that are molting. A millipede is very soft after it sheds its hard outer skin. It must wait for

Some types of millipedes make a special chamber for molting. It is made of soil and their own droppings.

the new armor to harden before it is safe again. But even after a millipede's armor hardens, predators love to catch them. Like an armadillo, only the top part of a millipede is protected by armor. Its belly is soft and unprotected.

Fortunately, millipedes have more protection than just their hard armor. They have several other tricks to use. Like the

▼ When threatened, a millipede can roll itself into a tiny, armored ball. This protects its soft belly.

three-banded armadillo, the millipede can roll up into a tight ball. This helps keep its soft belly safe. Some predators have even learned how to get around this, however. A mongoose, for example, knows how to smash the millipede against a rock to break its armor.

Wild FACT Another armored animal that can roll into a ball is the pill bug. It is also sometimes called a roly-poly or a doodlebug.

Many millipedes also have chemical defenses. They can make an oozy liquid that stinks. Most predators will leave the stinky millipede alone. Some millipedes can even produce poison. These poisons can do many things. Some simply sting or burn. There are even millipedes that have a poison that can make a small predator fall asleep! This gives the millipede time to get away.

Sticky Toes?

The palmetto tortoise beetle has a dome of armor on its back. It looks like a tiny, walking crash helmet. These dark-purple beetles can be found in the southeastern United States, in places such as Florida and Texas. Palmetto tortoise beetles live anywhere that palmetto plants grow, since that is their favorite food.

This beetle has more than just its armor for protection. When the palmetto tortoise beetle is attacked, it sticks tight to whatever leaf it is eating at the time. It has special feet that make the beetle almost impossible to move. These feet have thousands of tiny, sticky bristles, as well as an oily

liquid on them. This helps the palmetto tortoise beetle clamp down tightly and stick to a leaf.

Once the beetle is stuck, it can take a lot of pulling and tugging from a predator. No matter how hard an animal pulls, the beetle will not budge. Most predators give up and find food somewhere else. When the coast is clear, the palmetto tortoise beetle pops back up and keeps on eating.

Other millipedes' poisons are stronger, and can even kill small predators. These strong poisons are not enough to harm large predators such as birds. They are also usually not very harmful to humans. Against most predators, however, a millipede's super-tough armor is enough to keep it safe.

Armor for All

Going through life like a tough armored tank can be great for an animal. Its armor can keep it safe wherever it goes. Armored animals do not face as much danger from the sharp teeth of many predators. They are able to withstand many attacks that would kill other animals. Whether the armor is tough skin, bone, or stiff scales, it can give an animal the extra protection it needs to survive and can be an amazing animal defense.

People have used armor for thousands of years. Ancient humans learned much about armor from animals. They even used tough animal skins, skulls, and bones for protection during battle. Then humans discovered metal. They found that it made great armor. It also made better weapons.

Over the years, armor has changed as weapons have changed. Armor had to be built tougher as weapons became more deadly. Fighters wearing animal skin or bones would be no match for metal weapons such as swords.

The same is true today. Weapons are still changing. They have become far more deadly. Metal swords and spears are gone. Guns, rockets, and bombs have taken their place. It has been important

for armor to change also. Soldiers and police officers who face these deadly weapons need armor that is better than ever.

One of the big changes is the weight of the armor. If soldiers or police today had to wear clunky metal armor, they would never catch up with the bad guys. Soldiers and police have to be able to move fast. It is important to have light but tough body armor. The armor also needs to be comfortable and cool to wear.

That is where Kevlar comes in. This amazingly tough fiber was invented in the late 1960s. This material and others like it are used to make bulletproof vests (above). Kevlar is five times stronger than steel. It is super-strong but very lightweight. The Kevlar fibers are woven into a very tight "net" of fabric. There are many layers of this tight net in a bulletproof vest. These layers are the key to how Kevlar works.

The layers help spread the energy of a speeding bullet evenly through the vest. The more layers a vest has, the more powerful a bullet it can stop.

A person wearing a Kevlar vest is not completely free of injury when hit by a bullet, however. The force of a bullet as it hits the vest can still knock a person to the ground. The victim may suffer severe bruising or even a few broken ribs. But those are a small price to pay for surviving a gunshot.

Kevlar is also used to make armored helmets (below), and is used for gloves and on military vehicles. If soldiers or police need added protection, they can also use hard armor like ceramic. It can be used with soft armor like Kevlar for extra safety.

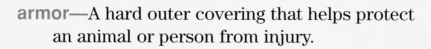

armor—A hard outer covering that helps protect an animal or person from injury.

burrow—Tunnel-like animal home under the snow or ground.

calcium carbonate—A powdery substance found in nature as chalk or limestone. It makes up the armor of some animals, such as snails.

carapace—A hard, protective shell-like covering of an animal.

carnivore—An animal that eats meat.

cephalothorax—The front section of animals such as spiders or crabs. It is made up of the head and thorax.

chitin—A tough, protective material that makes up the exoskeleton of some animals.

diplopods—A word meaning "double legged." A group of animals that includes millipedes. Each of their body segments has two pairs of legs attached.

exoskeleton—The hard outer covering of some animals that provides protection.

hydrothermal—Water heated naturally by the Earth.

keratin—A tough material that makes up hair, fingernails, hooves, feathers, and horns.

mammal—An animal with hair or fur. It usually gives birth to live young and is warm-blooded. It can also produce milk to feed its young.

molting—When an animal sheds its outer covering as it grows.

plastron—The underside part of a turtle's shell.

predator—An animal that hunts and eats other animals.

prey—An animal that is a food source for other animals.

reptile—One of a group of cold-blooded animals, including snakes, turtles, and lizards.

retractable—Able to be pulled back in.

scutes—Plates of keratin that cover a turtle's bony shell.

spawn—To produce offspring in large numbers.

telson—The last segment on the body of some animals, such as horseshoe crabs.

Books

Jango-Cohen, Judith. *Armadillos*. Tarrytown, N.Y.: Benchmark Books, 2004.

Laskey, Elizabeth. *Sea Turtles*. Chicago: Heinemann Library, 2003.

Mason, Paul. *Nature's Armor and Defenses*. Chicago: Heinemann-Raintree, 2007.

Internet Addresses

Biokids Critter Catalog: Millipedes
http://www.biokids.umich.edu/critters/Diplopoda/

Enchanted Learning: Horseshoe Crab
http://www.enchantedlearning.com/subjects/
invertebrates/arthropod/Horseshoecrab.shtml

Gulf of Maine Aquarium: All About Turtles
http://www.gma.org/turtles/index.html

National Geographic Animals: Armadillo
http://animals.nationalgeographic.com/animals/
mammals/armadillo.html

Index